Pet Care

# Gerbils

# Rebecca Sjonger & Bobbie Kalman

Photographs by Marc Crabtree

 Crabtree Publishing Company

www.crabtreebooks.com

# Gerbils

## A Bobbie Kalman Book

Dedicated by Kathy Middleton
For my mother Ruth, a friend to all animals

**Editor-in-Chief**
Bobbie Kalman

**Writing team**
Rebecca Sjonger
Bobbie Kalman

**Substantive editor**
Kathryn Smithyman

**Editors**
Mollly Aloian
Amanda Bishop
Kelley MacAulay

**Art director**
Robert MacGregor

**Design**
Margaret Amy Reiach

**Production coordinator**
Heather Fitzpatrick

**Photo research**
Crystal Foxton
Kristina Lundblad

**Consultant**
Dr. Michael A. Dutton, DVM, DABVP
Exotic and Bird Clinic of New Hampshire
www.exoticandbirdclinic.com

**Special thanks to**
Devan Cruickshanks, Brody Cruickshanks, Heather and Tim
Cruickshanks, Steve Cruickshanks, Kyle Foxton, Doug Foxton,
Aimee Lefebvre, Alissa Lefebvre, Jacquie Lefebvre, Jeremy Payne,
Dave Payne, Kathy Middleton, Natasha Barrett, Mike Cipryk
and PETLAND

**Photographs**
Ian Beames/ardea.com: page 10
Marc Crabtree: back cover, title page, pages 3, 4, 5, 6, 7, 12, 13,
    14, 15, 16-17, 18, 19 (top), 21 (top), 22-23, 24, 25, 28, 30, 31
firstlight.ca: front cover (gerbils), page 11
Robert MacGregor: page 21 (bottom)
Other images by Comstock, Digital Stock, and PhotoDisc

**Illustrations**
All illustrations by Margaret Amy Reiach

**Digital prepress**
Embassy Graphics

**Printer**
Worzalla Publishing Company

## Crabtree Publishing Company

www.crabtreebooks.com        1-800-387-7650

| | | |
|---|---|---|
| PMB 16A | 612 Welland Avenue | 73 Lime Walk |
| 350 Fifth Avenue | St. Catharines | Headington |
| Suite 3308 | Ontario | Oxford |
| New York, NY | Canada | OX3 7AD |
| 10118 | L2M 5V6 | United Kingdom |

Cataloging-in-Publication Data
Sjonger, Rebecca.
  Gerbils / Rebecca Sjonger & Bobbie Kalman;
photographs by Marc Crabtree.
      p. cm. -- (Pet care series)
  Includes index.
  ISBN 0-7787-1752-6 (RLB) -- ISBN 0-7787-1784-4 (pbk.)
  1. Gerbils as pets--Juvenile literature. [1. Gerbils. 2. Pets.]
I. Kalman, Bobbie. II. Crabtree, Marc, ill. III. Title. IV. Series.
  SF459.G4S57 2004
  636.935'83--dc22

                                                    2003027236
                                                    LC

# Contents

# What are gerbils?

Gerbils are **mammals**. Mammals have fur or hair on their bodies. They also have backbones. Mother mammals make milk inside their bodies to feed their babies. Gerbils are part of a group of mammals called **rodents**. Most rodents have small bodies and sharp front teeth.

## A gerbil's body

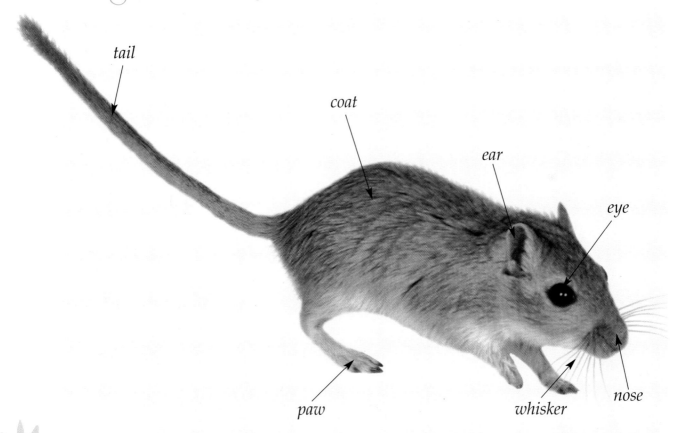

tail

coat

ear

eye

nose

whisker

paw

# Wild gerbils

**Wild gerbils**, or gerbils that are not pets, live in hot, dry areas. During the day, they sleep in underground tunnels called **burrows**. They leave their burrows to look for food after the hot sun goes down. In the 1950s, people started catching wild gerbils and keeping them as pets.

*Over time, most pet gerbils became active during the day as well as at night.*

# The right pet for you?

Gerbils are very curious animals. They love to explore and try new toys. You can spend hours watching your gerbil play. It will climb, jump, and dig its way around its cage! Owning a gerbil can be a lot of fun, but you also need to take very good care of it. You will have to feed your gerbil, clean its cage, and help it stay healthy.

*Your gerbil will learn to love spending time with you!*

# Are you ready?

The questions below will help
you and your family decide
if you are ready for a pet gerbil.

Do you have another pet,
such as a cat, that may
scare or hurt a gerbil?

Is there a quiet space in
your home where you
can put a cage?

Will you clean out the
cage at least once a week?

Who will feed the gerbil
and give it fresh water
every day?

Do you have time to
play with a gerbil
every day?

Is anyone in your family
**allergic** to gerbils?

# Plenty of gerbils

Only a few **breeds**, or kinds, of gerbils are kept as pets. Most pet gerbils are Mongolian gerbils. This kind of gerbil comes from the country of Mongolia in Asia. You may also see pet Egyptian gerbils, Shaw's **jirds**, and fat-tailed gerbils. Each breed looks and acts a bit differently.

*Mongolian gerbils are active during the day and at night. They are about eight inches (20 cm) long from the nose to the tip of the tail.*

*Egyptian gerbils are active mainly at night. They need to sleep during the day. Egyptian gerbils may bite when they are scared.*

*Shaw's jirds are friendly and smart. They are ideal pets!*

*Fat-tailed gerbils have very fat tails! They are known for being calm pets. You can play with them during the day or at night.*

## All mixed up!

The coats of most wild gerbils are a mix of brown and gray colors. At first, pet gerbils looked the same as wild gerbils. Then gerbils with different colored coats **mated** and had babies. Today, pet gerbils have coats that are black, brown, white, gray, and even blue!

# Baby gerbils

Baby gerbils are born in **litters**, or groups. Up to six **puppies**, or babies, may be born in one litter. When puppies are born, they have no fur. They cannot see or hear. Their mother protects and feeds them. She keeps her puppies together in a warm nest. Father gerbils also care for the babies.

*Puppies drink milk from their mother's body.*

## Be aware

If you let your gerbil mate and have babies, you will have a lot of little animals to care for! You must find good homes for the puppies before they grow up. Put male and female gerbils that are over three months old in separate cages to stop unwanted gerbils from being born.

## Growing up

After one week, most puppies have grown fur on their bodies. When the puppies are two weeks old, they can see and hear. They may also begin eating food other than milk. In just a few more weeks, they will be old enough to be separated into pairs and taken to new homes.

# Picking your gerbil

To find a pet gerbil, check your local **animal shelter**, or ask friends and family if they know of any gerbils that are being given away. You can also buy your gerbil from a pet store or a **breeder**. Make sure that you get your pet from people who take very good care of their animals.

*A gerbil that comes out of its hiding place to take a look at you will probably be happy around people.*

## Forever friends

Most gerbils enjoy the company of other gerbils. Gerbils from the same litter will get along very well. Choose a pair of gerbils that are both males or both females to avoid unwanted baby gerbils. If you get just one gerbil, you will need to give it a lot of attention to keep it from becoming lonely.

## What to look for

Take your time when you are picking the gerbil you want as your pet. Some of the ways you can tell if it is healthy are listed below.

 curious behavior

 a strong body

 a shiny, thick coat

 bright, clean eyes

 a clean nose and bottom and clean ears

 no sores or bald spots on its body

other healthy gerbils living in its cage

# Getting ready

Before you bring your gerbil home, get everything you need ready for your new pet. Some of the things that you will need to care for a gerbil are shown on these pages.

*If you are getting two gerbils, make sure that the cage has plenty of room for both.*

*Buy a bag of **bedding**, such as aspen shavings, for the bottom of the cage.*

*A small box or house gives your gerbil a dark, quiet place to hide when it is sleeping.*

*Give your gerbil branches from fruit trees to gnaw on and keep its teeth healthy.*

*Buy a **ceramic** food bowl. Your gerbil will not be able to tip it over or gnaw holes in it!*

*Get both fresh and packaged foods to keep your gerbil healthy.*

*A **salt lick** can give your gerbil the salt it needs in its diet.*

*A water bottle with a metal sipping tube will keep your gerbil's drinking water clean.*

*Get a few different toys to keep your gerbil active and happy!*

## Welcome home!

When you pick up your new gerbil, take along a carrying cage or a small cardboard box with air holes in it. Your pet can travel safely in the box. Visit a **veterinarian** or "vet" on your way home. Your vet will check the gerbil to make sure it is healthy. When you arrive at home, give your gerbil all the time it needs to get used to you and your family.

# Home sweet home

You can get a good cage for your gerbils at a pet store. Make sure plenty of fresh air can get into the cage. Most cages have plastic bases and wire mesh tops. If you buy a cage with a plastic bottom, pick one that has wires that go all the way to the bottom of the cage. Without the wires, your gerbil may escape by gnawing through the plastic! Your gerbil may also try to escape through the wires, so make sure the spaces between the wires are smaller than your gerbil is.

*Hard plastic tunnels may be fun for your gerbil. Make sure the tunnels have enough small air holes so that your gerbil can breathe when it goes inside!*

*A second level in the cage gives your gerbil more space.*

*Putting the water bottle outside the cage leaves more room inside for your gerbil.*

*Cover the cage floor with at least one inch (2.5 cm) of bedding. Avoid cedar and pine shavings—these woods could make your pet very sick!*

## The perfect place

Some of the things to look for when picking the best spot to put your gerbil's cage are listed below.

- quiet so your gerbil can sleep

- no direct sunlight

- a comfortable temperature between 65°F and 80°F (18°C to 26°C)

- not overly **humid**

# Gerbil food

Gerbils need a variety of foods to stay healthy. You can buy food made just for gerbils at a pet store. Packaged gerbil food is a mixture of nuts, grains, seeds, and dried vegetables. Read the label to find out how much to give your gerbil. Fresh fruits and vegetables will help your gerbils get a good balance of **nutrients** in their diet. A little less than a handful of chopped broccoli, celery, carrots, pears, bananas, or grapes will be a tasty treat for your gerbil!

*Most gerbils love sunflower seeds. Make sure your gerbil eats more than just sunflower seeds, though! It needs a variety of foods to be healthy.*

## Fresh water

Drinking clean water will help keep your gerbil healthy. Make sure your gerbil's bottle is always full of water. Wash and rinse the water bottle every day. Check it for leaks or cracks when you fill it back up.

## Not on the menu

Be very careful when you choose which foods to give your gerbil. Some foods can make your pet very sick!

Fruits and vegetables that have not been rinsed properly may have **pesticides** on the skins.

**Citrus fruits**, such as oranges or grapefruits, can make your gerbil ill.

Never give your gerbil rotten food. Take old food out of the cage every day.

Candy and sugary treats are not healthy for your gerbil.

Eating **dairy foods**, such as milk or ice cream, can make your gerbil sick.

# Gerbil grooming

Gerbils are clean animals. They spend a lot of time **grooming**, or cleaning, their bodies. Your gerbil uses its paws and teeth to keep its coat clean and looking good. Digging and gnawing help keep its teeth and claws short. Your pet may need your help with grooming, though.

## In the sandbox

Your gerbil will love taking a bath. Do not start filling up the tub with water, though! Your gerbil should bathe in a bowl or a box filled with clean sand. Rolling and playing in the sand helps clean dirt off its fur coat.

# Terrific teeth

Gerbils have four **incisors**, or sharp front teeth, which never stop growing. Gnawing helps grind down a gerbil's teeth and keeps them from getting too long. Your gerbil will gnaw on just about anything!

*Gnawing on fruit-tree wood keeps a gerbil's incisors short and healthy.*

# Clicky claws

Older gerbils may grow long claws as they become less active. If your gerbil's claws grow so long that they begin to curl, ask your veterinarian to show you how to trim them. You must be very careful because if the claws are cut too short, they may bleed.

*Always use scissors or clippers that are made just for trimming rodent claws.*

# Handle with care

Give your gerbil a day or two to explore its cage and begin to feel at home. You can then train it to be **handled**, or picked up. Always wash your hands before and after handling your gerbil. Follow the steps on these pages to help your pet get used to being picked up.

*Never pick up a gerbil by its tail, which can snap right off!*

## Hand training

Your gerbil needs to get used to your smell. Let it sniff your fingers and hands. You can hold out a few seeds to attract your gerbil's interest. Do not always offer food, though, or your gerbil will always want treats!

## Handy gerbils

Once your gerbil has had a few days to get used to the smell of your hand, it may climb onto your palm. You can let your gerbil travel from hand to hand so that it can move around. If you pick it up, be very careful to hold its body gently but firmly.

*Your gerbil may fall or jump out of your hand. It may get hurt if it falls a long distance to the ground! Keep your hand close to the floor or near a tabletop.*

# Play time!

Gerbils are very active animals. They love climbing, digging, hiding, and running. Make sure there are enough things for your gerbil to do in its cage. These pages show some common gerbil toys that you may want to include in your gerbil's home.

*Cardboard tubes make great tunnels or ladders for your gerbil.*

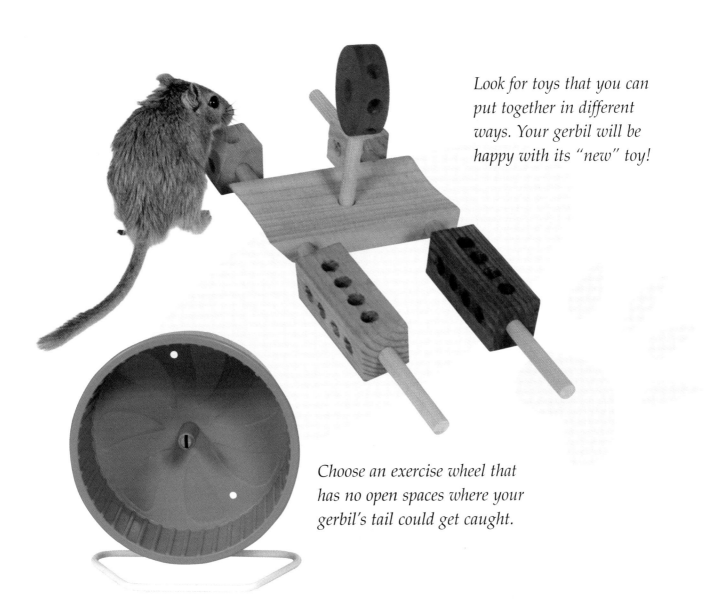

*Look for toys that you can put together in different ways. Your gerbil will be happy with its "new" toy!*

*Choose an exercise wheel that has no open spaces where your gerbil's tail could get caught.*

## One change at a time

Keep the cage interesting for your gerbil. Try adding new toys or moving toys from one area of the cage to another area. Take your time making changes, though. If you switch more than one toy at a time, your gerbil may become confused.

# Understanding your gerbil

Gerbils send messages to people and other animals. Watch how your gerbil moves its body. Listen for the sounds that it makes. Your pet may be trying to tell you something important! These pages show some of the ways that gerbils express themselves.

*Your gerbil will thump its back paws loudly when it gets excited or alarmed.*

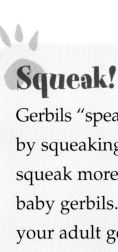

# Squeak!

Gerbils "speak" to one another by squeaking. Adult gerbils squeak more quietly than do baby gerbils. You may hear your adult gerbil squeak if it is scared or excited.

*A curious gerbil stands on its back legs and looks all around.*

*A scared gerbil also stands up on its back legs. It holds its paws together and its body becomes stiff.*

# Staying safe

Your gerbil will not bite you unless you have scared it. You can avoid being bitten by leaving your gerbil alone when it is sleeping. Remember to be gentle and careful when you are handling your pet. Never startle it when you pick it up! If your gerbil bites you, try not to drop it or squeeze it.

*Show your family and friends how to handle your gerbil properly.*

# Outdoor dangers

For gerbils, the outdoors can be a very dangerous place. Cats or birds may see a gerbil as a tasty treat! Never let your gerbil roam around outdoors. It may become scared and run away to a hiding place.

*Your pet cat may be the greatest danger to your gerbil!*

## Out and about

Before you let your gerbil out of its cage, look for these possible dangers.

- Are there doors or windows that your gerbil may use to escape?

- Are there any areas or furniture in which your gerbil might hide?

- Is there anything in the room that your gerbil may damage with its teeth or claws?

- Are there **poisonous** plants that your gerbil can reach and eat?

- Are there exposed electrical cords that may harm your gerbil if it bites them?

# Visiting a vet

A veterinarian is a medical doctor who treats animals. He or she will help you keep your gerbil healthy. If you think that your gerbil may be sick, take it to see a vet right away. Your gerbil has a better chance of surviving an illness if it is treated right away!

*If you ever have any questions about your gerbil's health, your vet can answer them for you.*

# When to get help

It is very important to take your gerbil to a vet at the first signs of an illness. Watch for any of the warning signs listed below.

- sleeping more than usual
- eating less food than usual
- runny eyes or nose
- sores or scabs on its skin
- fur becoming dull and thin
- heavy, loud breathing
- a wet bottom

# A great life

Your gerbil will live three to five years. Enjoy all the time you have with your pet! If you take very good care of it and treat it well, your gerbil will have a great life with you.

# Words to know

Note: Boldfaced words that are defined in the book may not appear on this page.

**allergic** Describing someone who has a physical reaction to something such as a food or animal dander

**animal shelter** A center that houses and cares for animals that do not have owners

**breeder** A person who brings gerbils together so the gerbils can make babies

**ceramic** Describing something that is made out of baked clay

**citrus fruit** Juicy fruit that has a thick skin, such as an orange

**dairy food** Food made with milk and milk products

**humid** Describing air that contains water vapor, which makes the air damp or moist

**jird** Another name for a gerbil

**mate** To join together to make babies

**nutrient** Material needed by a body to grow and stay healthy

**pesticide** Chemical made to kill insects

**poisonous** Describing something that has substances in it that may harm or kill an animal

**veterinarian** A medical doctor who treats animals

# Index

1 2 3 4 5 6 7 8 9 0  Printed in the U.S.A.  3 2 1 0 9 8 7 6 5 4